KB276125

Skis, Sleds, and Skates!

Happy House

About Wise & Wide

- A systematic 6-level English reading program based on Lexile® measures
- Diverse and interesting topics chosen from the elementary curriculums of Korea and English speaking western countries
- Well-written books in various forms including fiction stories, descriptive texts, and classics retold
- The informative but original fiction stories grab your interest, leading to the easy and clear understanding of the educational content.
- Improve thinking skills with solid after-reading activities at all levels of the series.

Wise & Wide is a 6-level English reading program that consists of 60 books and each level is systematically divided by Lexile® measures. The Lexile® Framework for Reading is the most popular reading measuring system in American formal education curriculums and many English programs. Over 20 out of 50 states in the U.S. mark Lexile® measures directly on students' final report cards and over 300 well-known publishers adopt and use Lexile® measures.

Experience many kinds of readings written by professional writers from the U.S. and England. They used interesting topics that were carefully chosen after analyzing elementary curriculums from around the world including Korea, the U.S., England, and Australia among many others. Comprehensive after-reading activities including graphic organizers, speaking tasks, and After-reading Tests are ready for you.

Levels in the series and their corresponding Lexile® measures

Level	Lexile® measures	U.S. Grade
Level 1	Below 200L	Pre K - K
Level 2	190L - 400L	Lower Grade 1
Level 3	350L - 530L	Upper Grade 1
Level 4	420L - 650L	Grade 2
Level 5	520L - 940L	Grade 3 - 4
Level 6	830L - 1070L	Grade 5 - 6

* Smart Readers: Wise & Wide level 1 is applicable to the preschool level in the U.S.

* The source of the relationship between Lexile® measures and U.S. school grades: CCSS(Common Core State Standards) FOR ENGLISH LANGUAGE ARTS, APPENDIX A (2012, which is used by 45 states in the U.S.)

Topic List

	Level 1	Level 2	Level 3	Level 4	Level 5	Level 6
Book 1	Science>Biology: The hibernation of animals Story	Science>Biology: Living and nonliving things Story	Science>Biology> Animals & the Environment: Sea otters Story	Environment> Living with nature: The diver & the persimmon tree Story	Science>Biology> Animal: Amazing animals of the Amazon Story	Science>Biology: Germs, transmitted diseases Story
Book 2	Literature> World classics: Aesop's fables Story	Literature> Traditional fairy tale: Old tales about stones Story	Social Studies> Economy: To run a business to make and save money Story	Science>Biology> Plants: Photosynthesis Story	Science>Earth science: Earth's layers, earthquakes, volcanoes, and earth's atmosphere Report	Mathematics> Sequence: The golden ratio & the Fibonacci sequence Story
Book 3	Science>Physics: How shadows are formed Story	Literature> World classics: Peter Pan Story	Science>Scientific technology: Nanobots Story	Literature>Myths: World's creation stories Story	Literature> Legend: The story of King Arthur Story	Literature>Myths: Constellation myths Story
Book 4	Literature> Traditional literature: The Talmud Story	Science>Biology> Animal: Polar bears Story	Science>Biology> Animal: Mountain gorillas Story	Social Studies> Cultural anthropology: Amazing ancient cultures of the world Story	Science> Earth science: Clouds and weather Story	Literature> Human & animals: The friendship between a girl and a horse Story
Book 5	Social Studies> Ethics: Rules in daily life Story	Science>Biology: The five senses Report	Social Studies> Cultural anthropology: Astonishing festivals Report	Art>Music: Stories from two operas Story	Social Studies> World culture & history: The Renaissance Story	Sports> Board sports: Surfing & snowboarding Story
Book 6	Social Studies> World geography & travel: Tourist attractions around the world Story	Science>Biology> Animal: Dinosaurs Story	Science> Astronomy: The solar system Story	Social Studies> People: Three great people who overcame hardships Story	Science>Scientific technology: The wonderful world of robots Report	Art>Music: Composers of the Romantic Era Report
Book 7	Science> Space science: The life of astronauts Report	Social Studies> Cultural anthropology: Mythological monsters from around the world Report	Mathematics> Elementary mathematics: Numbers, measurement, shapes and data Report	Science & Social Studies> Technology & culture: Inventions from around the world Report	Art>Works of art: Famous paintings Report	Social Studies> Human & animals: Animals in action for human Report
Book 8	Social Studies> Cultural anthropology: Various living cultures of the world Story	Art>Music: Instruments in the orchestra Story	Social Studies> Life safety: Learning and using outdoor survival skills Story	Social Studies> History: The California Gold Rush Report	Social Studies & Science> Psychology: Psychology in everyday life Story	Literature> World classics: The Merchant of Venice Story
Book 9	Social Studies> Jobs: Interviews about jobs Report	Science>Scientific technology: Developments in technology in different times Story	Social Studies> Politics>Election: Running for 3rd grade class president Story	Literature> World classics: Stories of Sherlock Holmes Story	Literature> World classics: Adrift in the Pacific Story	Social Studies> History & People: Great world leaders in history Report
Book 10	Literature>Traditional fairy tale: Eastern and Western folk tales on the same theme Story	Sports>Winter sports: Various aspects of some Winter Olympic sports Report	Literature> World classics: Short stories by O. Henry Story	Sports> Ball games: Various aspects of popular ball games Report	Social Studies> History: Famous events that changed world history Report	Art & Social Studies> Art: Stories about the creation, distribution, and preservation of paintings Report

* 10 books in each level will be published.

How to Use This Book

•Before Reading

You can easily find the topic and what kind of story you are about to read.

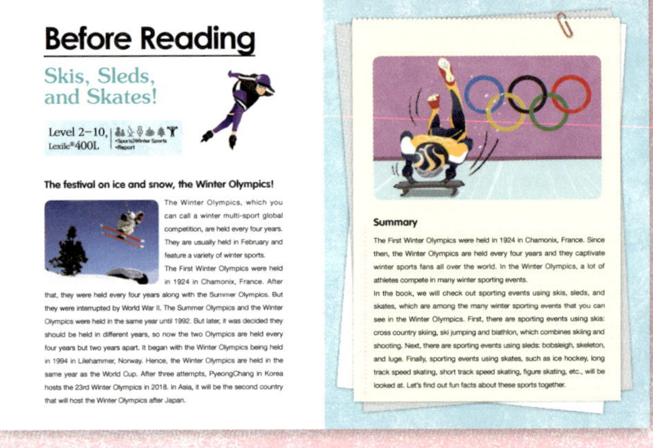

•The text

All the stories were written by professional writers from the U.S. and England, so you will read authentic and appropriate English sentences and expressions in every book in the series.

•Pop Quiz

Check out right away if you understand what you have just read by solving a pop quiz that checks your comprehension.

•Key Words

The key words and expressions on each page are listed for you to easily study them.

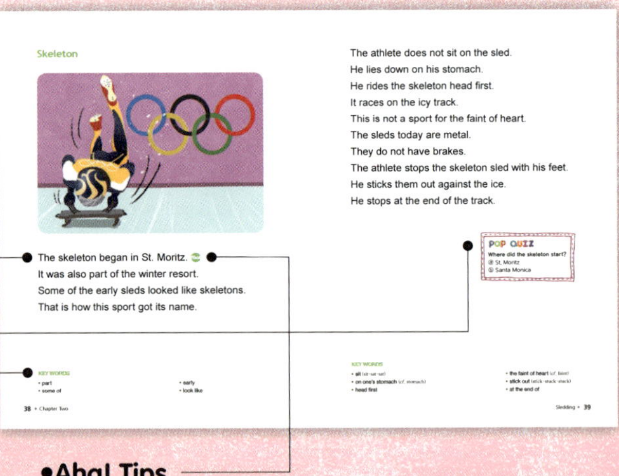

•Aha! Tips

Download free Korean explanations at *www.ihappyhouse.co.kr* for all of the sentences marked with "Aha!". These explain cultural, scientific, and economic knowledge or they deal with aspects of English such as grammatical structures or idiomatic expressions. There are lots of "Aha! Tips" to help you understand the text.

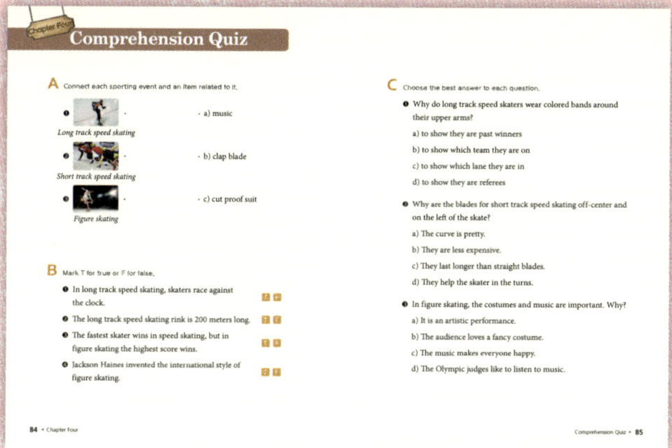

•Comprehension Quiz

After reading one chapter, solve various questions to find out if you fully understand the content.

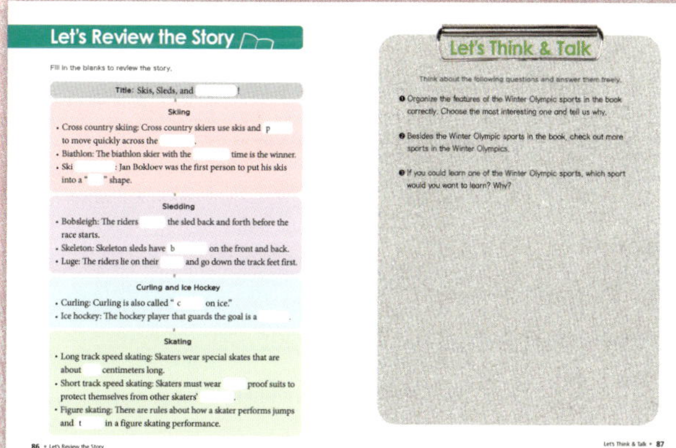

•Let's Review the Story /
•Let's Think & Talk

Fill in the blanks in the organizer to summarize the whole story. Express your own thinking and feelings about the story by answering the questions. You can build up logic and reasoning skills for your essay examinations in the future.

Appendix

Audio CD

In the CD audio book form, the texts are read vividly by American professional voice actors. (MP3 files downloaded for free)

After-reading Test

Solve an additionally provided After-reading Test for each book.

The Korean translation, Answer Keys, a Word Quiz, a Word List, and Aha! Tips for each book

You can download them for free at *www.ihappyhouse.co.kr* or *www.darakwon.co.kr*

Before Reading

Skis, Sleds, and Skates!

Level 2–10,
Lexile® 400L

•Sports⟩Winter Sports
•Report

The festival on ice and snow, the Winter Olympics!

The Winter Olympics, which you can call a winter multi-sport global competition, are held every four years. They are usually held in February and feature a variety of winter sports.

The First Winter Olympics were held in 1924 in Chamonix, France. After that, they were held every four years along with the Summer Olympics. But they were interrupted by World War II. The Summer Olympics and the Winter Olympics were held in the same year until 1992. But later, it was decided they should be held in different years, so now the two Olympics are held every four years but two years apart. It began with the Winter Olympics being held in 1994 in Lilehammer, Norway. Hence, the Winter Olympics are held in the same year as the World Cup. After three attempts, PyeongChang in Korea hosts the 23rd Winter Olympics in 2018. In Asia, it will be the second country that will host the Winter Olympics after Japan.

Summary

The First Winter Olympics were held in 1924 in Chamonix, France. Since then, the Winter Olympics are held every four years and they captivate winter sports fans all over the world. In the Winter Olympics, a lot of athletes compete in many winter sporting events.

In the book, we will check out sporting events using skis, sleds, and skates, which are among the many winter sporting events that you can see in the Winter Olympics. First, there are sporting events using skis: cross country skiing, ski jumping and biathlon, which combines skiing and shooting. Next, there are sporting events using sleds: bobsleigh, skeleton, and luge. Finally, sporting events using skates, such as ice hockey, long track speed skating, short track speed skating, figure skating, etc., will be looked at. Let's find out fun facts about these sports together.

Contents

Skis, Sleds, and Skates!

Skis, Sleds, and Skates!

Skiing and Shooting

Do you enjoy sports?

People all around the world do.

The Olympics are a way to celebrate sports.

The First Winter Olympics were in 1924.

They were named "Winter Sports Week."

There were nine different sports.

They had different types of skiing.

They had sledding and skating.

They had curling.

There was ice hockey, too.

In today's Olympics, there are many more sports.

Let's look at some interesting winter sports.

KEY WORDS

- skiing
- shooting
- **do** (do-did-done)
- enjoy
- all around the world
- the Olympics
  (= the Olympic Games)
- way
- celebrate

- first
- be named
  (*cf.* name)
- **Week** (*cf.* week)
- different
- type
- sledding
- skating
- curling

- ice hockey
- too
- today
- many more
- let's + *Verb*
- look at
- some
- interesting

Cross Country

In Norway, people have always skied.

They ski to gather firewood in the winter.

They ski to hunt for food.

They ski across the snow to visit friends.

The word "ski" comes from Norway.

It means "a strip of wood."

Skiers move across the snow and use poles to

help themselves go faster.

The first skis were strips of wood.

Skis today are different.

They are longer.

They have curved tips.

KEY WORDS

- cross country
- Norway
- always
- ski
- gather
- firewood
- hunt
- **across the snow** (*cf.* across)
- visit
- friend
- word
- **come from** (come-came-come)

- **mean** (mean-meant-meant)
- strip
- wood
- skier
- move
- use
- pole
- help
- faster
- longer
- **curved** (*cf.* curve)
- tip

Cross country is the oldest form of skiing. **Aha!**

Cross country ski boots are a bit like running shoes.

Skiers have two long poles. They use them to push themselves over the snow. They wear special suits.

They are like runners' clothes.

The suits hug skiers' bodies.

This helps them ski fast.

Cross country ski races started in the 1800s.

The first one was in 1842.

In the First Winter Olympics, cross country skiing was only for men.

In the 1952 Olympics, women began to compete.

Cross country ski races can be long or short.

Short races are 5 kilometers.

Long races can be 50 kilometers.

The winner is the fastest skier.

Who is the winner of the cross country ski race?
ⓐ the strongest skier
ⓑ the fastest skier

KEY WORDS

- race
- start
- only
- men (*cf.* women)

- **begin** (begin-began-begun)
- **compete**
- **can + *Verb***
- **kilometer** (1 km = 1,000 m)

- **winner**
- **fastest**

Biathlon

The biathlon has skiing and shooting. (Aha!)

The oldest pictures of the biathlon are in Norway.

They are on rock carvings.

They are thousands of years old.

The carvings show men on skis hunting animals.

This sport has been around for a long time!

At first, the biathlon was called Military Patrol.

Norway used it to protect the country.

Soldiers trained hard.

▲ an image of the biathlon carved on a rock

POP QUIZ

What was the first name for the biathlon?
ⓐ Military Patrol
ⓑ Shoot and Ski

KEY WORDS

- biathlon
- picture
- rock
- carving
- thousands of years

- around
- for a long time
- at first
- be called
- military patrol (*cf.* military / patrol)

- protect
- country
- soldier
- train
- hard

In 1767, two different companies protected the borders of Sweden and Norway.

They had a contest.

This may have been the first biathlon contest.

In the 1930s, the Finnish army defended itself against the Russian army by skiing fast and shooting well. Aha!

▲ Finnish ski troops during the war between Finland and Russia
(By Official Finnish photograph [Public domain or Public domain],
via Wikimedia Commons)

In 1861, a ski club started in Norway.

It was called the Trysil Ski and Rifle Club.

The club made the biathlon a sport.

Teams had four men.

They used wooden skis.

They shot military rifles.

The rifles were heavy.

Skiers carried them strapped on their backs.

Teams had to ski fast and shoot well.

▲ skiers with rifles on their backs
(See page for author [Public domain], via Wikimedia Commons)

Today, the skis are not wood.
They are made in a new way.
Now skis are lighter and
faster on the snow.
The bindings are narrow
and light.

▲ ski bindings

They send energy from the feet into the skis.

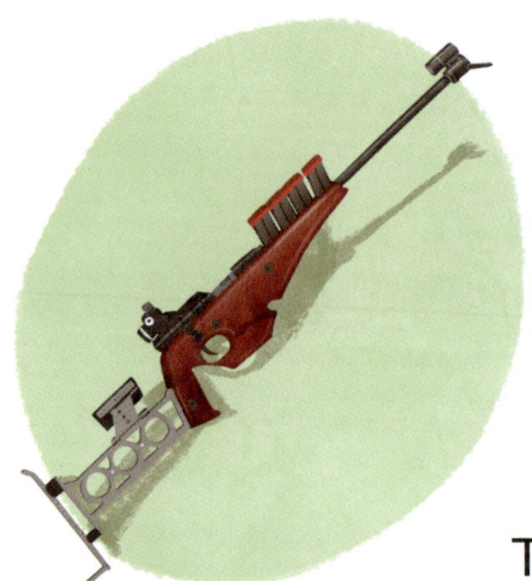

This extra push makes
skiers glide across the
snow faster than ever. **Aha!**
The rifles are different
today, too.
They are sport rifles.
They shoot in very cold
weather, even 20 degrees below zero.

KEY WORDS

- lighter
- binding
- narrow
- **send** (send-sent-sent)
- energy

- from A (in)to B (*cf.* into)
- feet
- extra
- glide
- than

- ever
- weather
- even
- degree
- below zero

The first targets were glass.

Then they were metal.

Next, the targets were paper.

Now the targets are mechanical.

When a target is hit, it flips from black to white.

In 1924, the targets were 250 meters away from the skier.

Today they are closer.

They are only 50 meters away.

▲ a target in a biathlon competition

KEY WORDS

- target
- glass
- then
- metal

- mechanical
- when
- **hit** (hit-hit-hit)
- flip

- **meter** (1m = 100cm)
- away
- closer

The skiers stop to shoot two or four times.

They stop at a shooting lane.

There are five targets in a shooting lane.

At some shooting lanes, the skiers must lie down.

At other shooting lanes, they must stand up.

If the skier misses the target, he gets a penalty.

He may have to ski an extra lap.

He may have one minute added to his time.

▲ (By Götz A. Primke from Muenchen, Germany (Biathlon_
WC_Antholz_2006_01_Film3_MassenDamen_13)
[CC BY-SA 2.0 (http://creativecommons.org/licenses/by-
sa/2.0)], via Wikimedia Commons)

KEY WORDS

- stop
- *Number* + times
- lane
- must + *Verb*
- lie down (lie-lay-lain)
- other
- stand up (stand-stood-stood)
- if

- miss
- get a penalty (get-got-gotten)
  (*cf.* penalty)
- lap
- minute
- add
- time

The biathlon was in the First Winter Olympics.

It became a medal event at the 1960 Winter Olympics.

Since 1992, women have been in the biathlon.

Today, biathlon races are short or long.

There are different types of races.

Some are 6 kilometers.

Some are as long as 20 kilometers. **Aha!**

The skier with the fastest time is the winner.

In Europe, the biathlon is the most popular winter sport on television.

KEY WORDS

- **become** (become-became-become)
- **medal**
- **event**
- **since**
- **as ... as ~** (*cf.* as)

- **Europe**
- **most**
- **popular**
- **on (the) television**

Ski Jumping

The military in Norway used skis.

One day, in 1808, a soldier named Olaf Rye was having some fun with friends.

He jumped 9.5 meters in the air.

Ski jumping was born. **Aha!**

Other skiers wanted to try it, too.

Soon it was a popular sport.

The first contest was held at the Trysil Ski and Rifle Club.

That was in 1862.

The First Winter Olympics had ski jumping.

▲ Olaf Rye
(By Aug. Jerndorff [Public domain],
via Wikimedia Commons)

KEY WORDS

- ski jumping
- one day
- have fun
- jump
- in the air
- be born
- want
- try
- soon
- be held
  (*cf.* hold (hold-held-held))

After World War I, a new method started.

It helped skiers jump farther.

Some jumped as far as 100 meters.

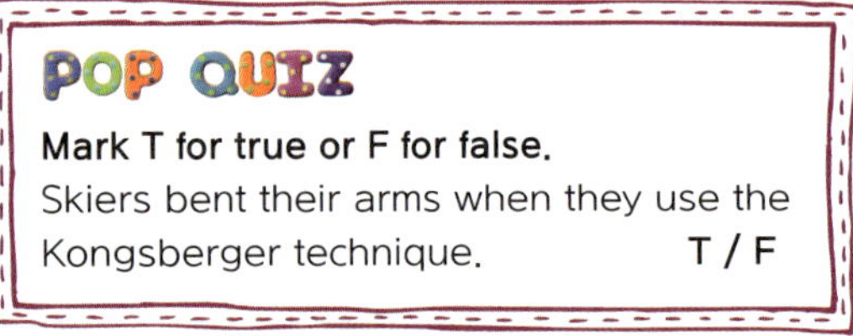

▲ (Deutsche Fotothek [CC BY-SA 3.0 de (http://creativecommons.org/licenses/by-sa/3.0/de/deed.en)], via Wikimedia Commons)

It was called the Kongsberger technique. Using this method, skiers bent forward at the hips. They kept their skis straight.

They spread their arms wide.

KEY WORDS

- after
- World War I
- method
- farther
- technique
- bend (bend-bent-bent)
- forward
- hip
- keep (keep-kept-kept)
- straight
- spread (spread-spread-spread)
- wide

Then, in 1985, a skier named Jan Bokloev did something different. **Aha!**

He pointed his skis into a "V" shape.

Some judges didn't like this idea.

They thought it did not look right.

But the new method was a success.

Jan jumped farther than ever.

By 1992, all Olympic ski jumpers did the "V."

▲ the V-style
(By Nelinjo (Own work) [CC BY-SA 4.0
(http://creativecommons.org/licenses/by-sa/4.0)],
via Wikimedia Commons)

KEY WORDS

- point
- shape
- judge
- idea
- think (think-thought-thought)
- right
- success
- jumper

Chapter One

Comprehension Quiz

A Mark T for true or F for false.

❶ The Olympics are a way to practice sports. **T F**

❷ Cross country ski races are as short as 5 km and as long as 50 km. **T F**

❸ The first name for the biathlon was Shoot and Ski. **T F**

❹ Norway, Sweden, and Finland used the biathlon to protect the borders of their countries. **T F**

B Fill in each blank with the right word(s) below.

jumping	Winter	"V" shape	shooting lane

❶ The First __________ Olympics took place in the year 1924.

❷ In the biathlon, skiers must ski fast and then stop to shoot in a __________.

❸ Ski __________ was born when a soldier named Olaf Rye was having fun with friends.

❹ Jan Bokloev pointed his skis into a __________.

 Choose the best answer to each question.

❶ What were the First Winter Olympics also named?

a) Winter Wonderland Sports

b) Winter Sports Week

c) Winter Outdoor Sports

d) Winter Olympic Week

❷ Which sport did the First Winter Olympics NOT have?

a) cross country skiing

b) biathlon

c) ice hockey

d) swimming

❸ What is the name of the technique in which skiers bend forward and keep their skis straight and their arms wide?

a) Axel technique

b) Kongsberger technique

c) Haines technique

d) Trysil technique

Sledding

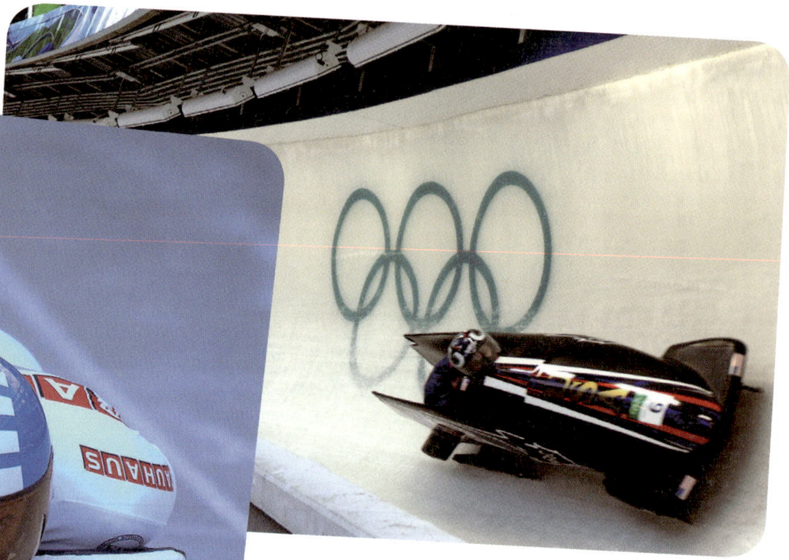

▲ (By Tim Hipps [Public domain], via Wikimedia Commons)

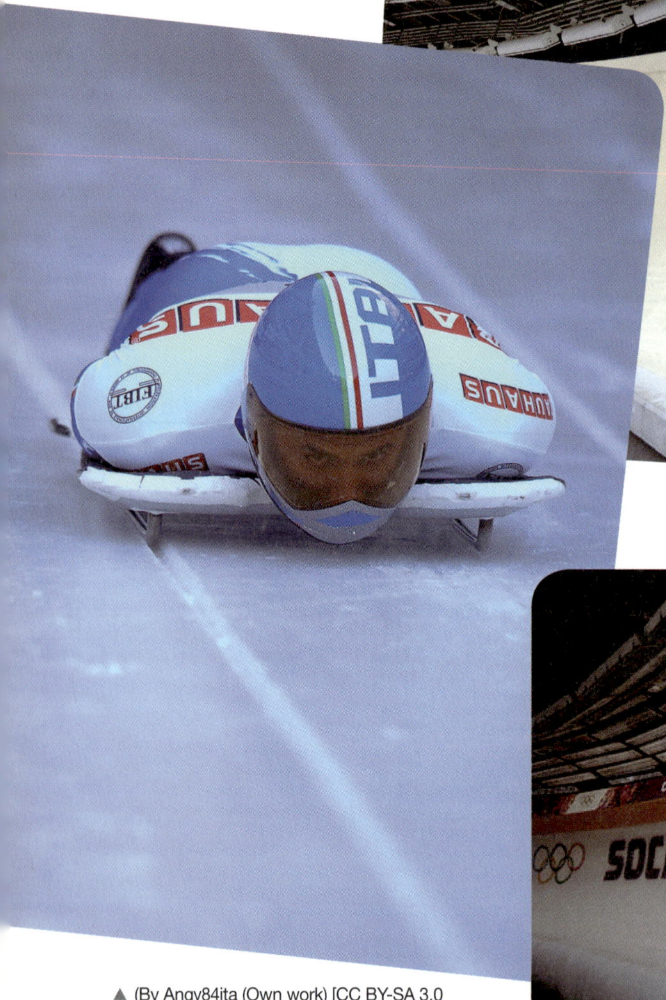

▲ (By Angy84ita (Own work) [CC BY-SA 3.0
(http://creativecommons.org/licenses/by-sa/3.0)],
via Wikimedia Commons)

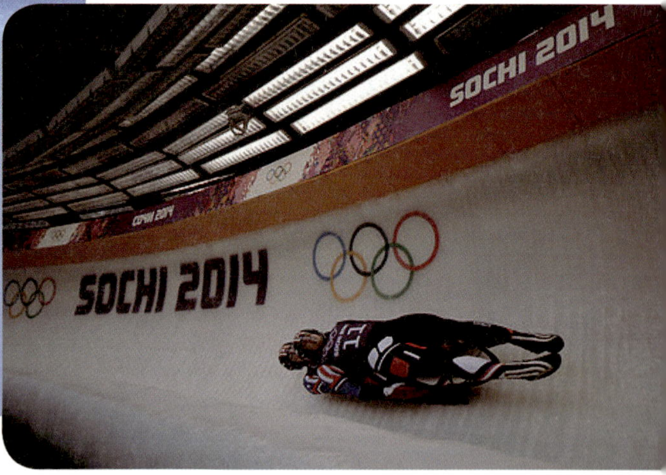

▲ (By The U.S. Army (Flickr: Luge doubles)
[CC BY 2.0 (http://creativecommons.org/licenses/by/2.0)],
via Wikimedia Commons)

Have you ever gone sledding?

The bobsleigh, skeleton, and luge are all similar to sledding.

These three sports began in Switzerland.

They were the idea of one man.

His name was Caspar Badrutt.

He owned a hotel in St. Moritz.

But he had a problem.

Everyone liked his hotel in the summer.

No one liked his hotel in the winter.

So he turned his hotel into a "winter resort."

He started new sports.

Rich people came to play.

KEY WORDS

- Have you ever + *p.p.*?
- bobsleigh
- skeleton
- luge
- be similar to
- own
- hotel
- St. Moritz
- problem
- everyone
- no one
- so
- turn A into B (*cf.* turn)
- resort
- rich
- come to play (*cf.* play)

Bobsleigh

One of the first sports was the bobsleigh. 

People strapped two sleds together.

Then, they zoomed down city streets.

They steered with ropes.

Sledding in the street was unsafe.

They decided to move the bobsleigh track.

They chose a track with natural ice.

It was on a hill.

It went down into the town of Cresta.

It was called the Cresta Run.

People rode their sleds down the hill on the twisting track.

KEY WORDS

- one of + *Plural Noun*
- sled
- together
- zoom down
- city
- street
- steer
- rope
- unsafe (↔ safe)
- decide
- track
- **choose** (choose-chose-chosen)
- natural
- hill
- **go down** (go-went-gone)
- **run** (run-ran-run)
- **ride** (ride-rode-ridden)
- twisting

▲ (By U.S. Navy photo by Journalist 1st Class Preston Keres. [Public domain], via Wikimedia Commons)

The first bobsleighs were made of wood.

(See page for author [Public domain], via Wikimedia Commons)

This made them heavy. Today, they are light and sleek. They are made of fiberglass and steel.

They have handles on the sides.

The athletes hold the handles.

Before the start, they bob the sled back and forth.

It helps them get a good start.

That is why it is called a bobsleigh.

KEY WORDS

- **be made of** (*cf.* make (make-made-made))
- **sleek**
- **fiberglass**
- **steel**
- **handle**
- side
- athlete
- bob
- back and forth
- that is why

▲ inside the bobsleigh

A bobsleigh has steering.

Each bobsleigh has two axles.

This helps to steer the sleigh around icy turns.

The bobsleigh also has a brake.

The brake is just a piece of metal.

It digs into the ice.

This slows the bobsleigh to a stop.

KEY WORDS

- steering
- each
- axle
- sleigh

- icy
- also
- brake
- just

- a piece of
- dig into (dig-dug-dug)
- slow

A team can have up to four people.

They wear safety helmets.

They wear special shoes.

The shoes have spikes on them.

The shoes grip the icy track.

The athletes bob, push, and run.

Then, they jump in.

They hang on tight!

The bobsleigh speeds down the icy track.

It goes up to 150 kilometers an hour.

The fastest team wins the race. `Aha!`

The bobsleigh was in the First Winter Olympics.

KEY WORDS

- up to
- safety helmet (*cf.* safety / helmet)
- spike
- grip
- jump in

- hang on tight (hang-hung-hung)
- speed
- hour (*cf.* an hour)
- win (win-won-won)

Skeleton

The skeleton began in St. Moritz. (Aha!)

It was also part of the winter resort.

Some of the early sleds looked like skeletons.

That is how this sport got its name.

- part
- some of

- early
- look like

The athlete does not sit on the sled.

He lies down on his stomach.

He rides the skeleton head first.

It races on the icy track.

This is not a sport for the faint of heart.

The sleds today are metal.

They do not have brakes.

The athlete stops the skeleton sled with his feet.

He sticks them out against the ice.

He stops at the end of the track.

KEY WORDS

- **sit** (sit-sat-sat)
- **on one's stomach** (*cf.* stomach)
- **head first**
- **the faint of heart** (*cf.* faint)
- **stick out** (stick-stuck-stuck)
- **at the end of**

Skeleton sleds today have bumpers.

The bumpers are on the front and back.

This protects the rider from the walls of the track.

Athletes wear special helmets.

They also wear racing suits.

Their shoes have spikes.

The spikes dig into the ice.

This helps in the running start.

▲ skeleton equipment

The skeleton used to be an event for men. **Aha!**

It was in the Olympics in 1928 and 1948.

After that, it was dropped.

It came back in 2002.

Now it is a sport for women, too.

Skeleton racers go very fast.

The fastest person wins the race.

KEY WORDS

- bumper
- on the front and back
- rider
- wall

- racing suit
- running start
- used to + *Verb*
- be dropped (*cf.* drop)

- come back
- racer
- person

Luge

▲ (By Jon Wick (http://www.flickr.com/photos/
jonwick/4363939510/)
[CC BY 2.0 (http://creativecommons.org/licenses/
by/2.0)], via Wikimedia Commons)

In the luge, athletes lie on their backs. 

They ride on a tiny sled.

They slide down the track feet first.

The bobsleigh and the luge use the same track.

The athletes wear a special helmet.

It has a visor that covers the chin.

They can look down over their chins.

They can see through the visor.

They can see the track.

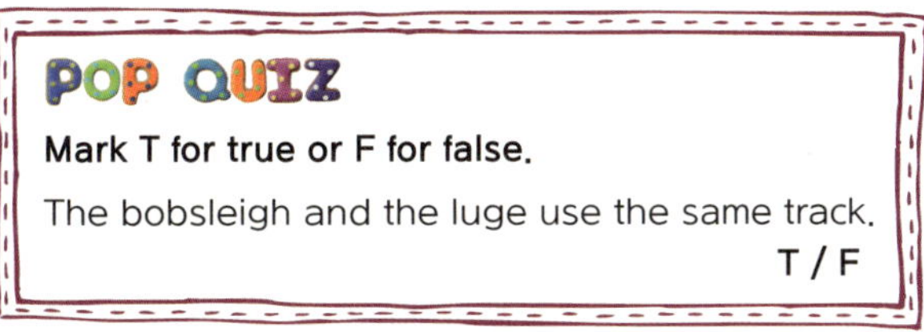

KEY WORDS

- on one's back
- tiny
- **slide** (slide-slid-slid/slidden)
- visor
- cover
- chin
- look down
- **see through** (see-saw-seen) (*cf.* through)

The athletes have special shoes with zippers.

They have to keep their feet pointed in the race.

The shoes help them do this.

The athletes steer with their feet.

They push against the sled runners.

Their gloves have spikes on them.

They push off against the ice with their hands.

Then, they grab the handles on the sides of the sled.

Down the track they go! **Aha!**

The one with the fastest time wins.

The first international luge race was in 1883.

The luge became an Olympic event in 1964.

Comprehension Quiz

A Mark T for true or F for false.

❶ The first bobsleighs were steered with ropes. T F

❷ The name of the first natural bobsleigh run was called the Cresta Run. T F

❸ A bobsleigh has one axle. T F

❹ Luge riders' gloves have spikes on them. T F

❺ The first international luge race was in 1964. T F

B Circle the right word(s) for each underlined part.

❶ A bobsleigh has a brake that (slides across / digs into) the ice.

❷ Bobsleigh riders wear shoes with (spikes / laces) on them.

❸ A person rides the skeleton lying on his (stomach / back).

❹ Athletes ride on a luge lying on their (backs / stomachs).

 Choose the best answer to each question.

❶ What is the greatest number of people that can be on a bobsleigh team?

a) 1

b) 2

c) 4

d) 6

❷ How does an athlete stop the skeleton?

a) He sticks his feet out.

b) He digs his gloves into the ice.

c) He hits a padded wall.

d) He pushes the brake.

❸ What is special about luge riders' shoes?

a) They have rubber on the bottom.

b) They have spikes for running.

c) They help the rider keep his feet pointed.

d) They have extra padding.

Curling Stones and Hockey Pucks

Curling Yesterday

Curling is an old game. 

Long ago, people played it in Scotland.

They played on frozen ponds.

People shoved big stones across the ice.

The stones made loud sounds.

They sounded like grumbling, rumbling, and roaring.

So curling got another name.

They called it the Roaring Game.

◀ (By Roger Griffith (Archival.) [Public domain], via Wikimedia Commons)

KEY WORDS

- puck
- yesterday
- long ago
- Scotland
- frozen
- pond
- shove
- make a sound
- loud
- sound like
- grumbling
- rumbling
- roaring
- another

The oldest curling stone is from 1511.

Now curling stones have metal handles.

Athletes must be very strong for curling.

They have to push the stones.

Each stone weighs 19.96 kilograms.

Now that is heavy!

The stones are made of special granite.

The granite comes from a place in Scotland.

It is called Ailsa Craig.

The curling stone is polished.

It is smooth.

This is the reason it can slide over the ice.

KEY WORDS

- weigh
- kilogram
- granite
- place
- Ailsa Craig
- polish
- smooth
- reason
- rink
- rectangle
- *Number* + meter(s) long
- *Number* + meter(s) wide

▲ ([Public domain], via Wikimedia Commons)

Today, curling is played on rinks.

The ice rink is a long rectangle.

It is 42.07 meters long.

It is 4.28 meters wide.

It has a target at the end of the rink.

The target is called a house.

Teams have four players.

The skip is the captain of the team.

The team works closely together.

They try to get their stones as close to the center of the house as they can.

They plan their game carefully.

▲ chess

Chess players plan their games, too. (Aha!) So curling has the nickname, "chess on ice."

The ice on the rink has tiny bumps.

It is called pebbled ice.

First, the ice is made flat and smooth.

Then, ice makers sprinkle water on the ice.

They use special tools.

This makes the pebbles.

They do this between each contest.

The pebbling helps the teams.

It helps the curling stone move.

As the stone moves across the pebbles, they melt.

This makes a thin layer of water on the ice.

The water helps the stone move.

It also gives it a spin.

The spin is called a curl.

That is why the sport is called curling.

One player is called the thrower.

He holds the stone by the handle.

He pushes it across the ice.

Two sweepers stay by the stone.

They sweep the ice in front of the stone.

They use brooms.

The brooms look like push brooms.

Sweeping the ice keeps the stone moving.

They may not touch the stone.

- melt
- thin
- layer
- spin
- curl

- thrower
  (*cf.* throw (throw-threw-thrown))
- sweeper
- stay
- **sweep** (sweep-swept-swept)

- in front of
- broom
- push broom
- touch

The skip watches the stone.

He yells to the sweepers.

He tells them where to move it.

The sweepers yell to the skip.

They tell him how fast the stone is moving.

They yell and sweep all the way to the target.

There are eight stones.

They do this eight times.

KEY WORDS

- watch
- yell
- where
- how fast

- all the way
- Canada
- French
- stick

- university
- write down
  (write-wrote-written)
- rule

Ice Hockey

Ice hockey started in
Canada in the 1800s. 
The name hockey comes
from a French word.
The word means "stick."
Two students at McGill University in Canada
wrote down the rules.

▲ an ice hockey game being played at McGill University
(By Notman & Son [Public domain or Public domain], via Wikimedia Commons)

A team has six
players on the ice.
The players skate
on an ice rink.
They use sticks to
pass and shoot a
small disk.
The disk is called a puck.

They get a point
when the puck
goes into a goal.
The goal is a cage
with a net.
The goalie tries to
stop the puck from
going into the goal. Aha!
Each team protects its goalie.

KEY WORDS

- skate
- disk
- goal

- cage
- net
- goalie

- have a break
- again

An ice hockey game is sixty minutes long.

Teams play for twenty minutes.

Then, they have a break.

Then, they play again.

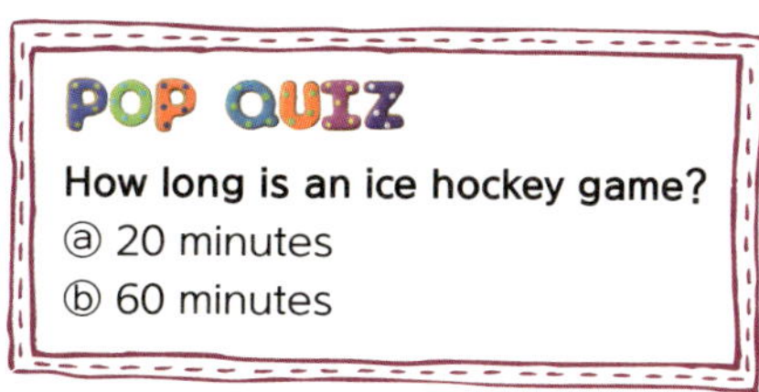

The players wear helmets.

They wear shin guards and elbow pads.

They wear gloves and face guards.

The goalie wears a face mask.

This is because the game moves fast.

Players can get hurt.

▲ ice hockey player clothing

▲ ice hockey goalie clothing

Men's ice hockey was in the 1920 Summer Olympics.

Men's ice hockey was also in the First Winter Olympics in 1924.

At the 1998 Winter Olympics, women got to do curling and play ice hockey, too.

Comprehension Quiz

A Mark T for true or F for false.

❶ The oldest curling stone ever found is from the year 1511.　　T　F

❷ Curling stones are made of a special kind of rock called granite.　　T　F

❸ The word hockey means "pole."　　T　F

B Fill in each blank with the right word below.

sweepers	house	bumps	puck

❶ The curling team pushes the stone to the target. The target is called the __________.

❷ Pebbled ice is ice that has tiny __________.

❸ A __________ is the disk players use in a hockey game.

❹ The curling team has a captain called the skip, a player called the thrower, and two players called __________.

C Choose the best answer to each question.

❶ Why is curling called "The Roaring Game"?

    a) The two teams roar at each other while they play.

    b) The curling stones make a roaring sound as they slide on the ice.

    c) The stones roar when they hit each other.

    d) The crowd roars when a game finishes.

❷ What does an ice hockey goal look like?

    a) a glass box

    b) a round hoop

    c) a cage with a net

    d) a hole in the ice

❸ How does a hockey team score a point?

    a) They shot the puck into the goal.

    b) The hit a home run.

    c) They return a serve.

    d) The other team makes a foul.

Three Kinds of Skating

What did Marie Antoinette and Napoleon III both like to do? **Aha!**

They loved to skate.

Perhaps you do, too.

Skating is an old sport.

In Holland, people used to skate on frozen waterways.

They were like streets in the winter.

People had skating contests.

They did this for hundreds of years.

Later, skating became popular in England.

People formed skating clubs and rinks.

KEY WORDS

- kind
- both
- perhaps
- Holland

- waterway
- hundreds of years
- later

Long Track Speed Skating

Ice speed skating is a very old sport. Aha!
Outdoor skating races were held in the 1800s.
At the First Winter Olympics in 1924, speed
skaters raced outdoors.

KEY WORDS

• speed skating   • **outdoor** (*cf.* outdoors)   • skater

Today, most races are on an indoor rink.

It is 400 meters long.

The athletes can race in teams.

They race against the clock.

Some skaters start on the outside of the track.

They wear colored armbands.

The color shows what lane they are in.

Other skaters start on the inside of the track.

They wear different colored armbands.

Skaters wear racing suits.

This helps them go faster.

KEY WORDS

- indoor (↔ outdoor)
- against the clock
- on the outside of
- colored
- armband
- on the inside of

The skates are about 42 centimeters long.

They have a special blade.

It is called a clap blade.

▲ the clap blade

(It allows the blade to remain in contact with the
ice longer, so it increases propulsive force.)

It has a hinge.

The skater lifts a foot.

The blade stays on the ice.

The skater puts a foot back down.

The blade snaps into place.

It makes a sound like a clap.

The clap blade helps the skater go faster.

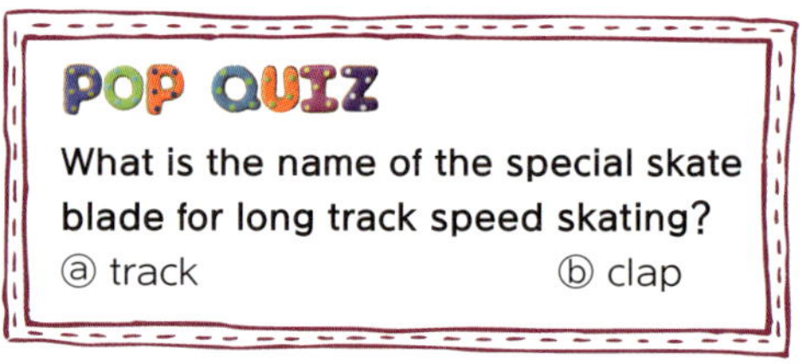

KEY WORDS

- about
- centimeter
- blade
- clap
- hinge
- lift
- snap
- into place

Skaters may wear helmets.

They may wear a hood instead.

They usually wear goggles.

This protects their eyes from ice chips.

They may wear gloves.

Short Track Speed Skating

▲ (By Noelle Neu (Link to posting of image) [GFDL (http://www.gnu.org/copyleft/fdl.html) or CC-BY-SA-3.0 (http://creativecommons.org/licenses/by-sa/3.0/)], via Wikimedia Commons)

In the early 1900s, there were no long tracks in Canada.

So they used small ice skating rinks.

That is how short track speed skating began. 

KEY WORDS

- short track
- sharp turn
- be different from

- at the same time
- sometimes
- bump into

- each other
- crash into

The short track is 111.12 meters long.

It has sharp turns.

This is different from a long track.

Many skaters race at the same time.

Sometimes they bump into each other.

Sometimes they crash into a wall.

The walls of the rinks are padded.

This helps skaters not to get hurt.

Short track skaters must wear helmets.

They wear goggles.

They wear elbow and knee guards.

They wear racing suits.

They wear gloves.

The suits and gloves are cut proof.

This protects them from other racers' skate blades.

Short track skates are different from long track skates. The blades are off center. They are to the left.

KEY WORDS

- knee
- cut proof (*cf.* proof)
- be off center
- to the left (*cf.* left)

The skater can dig into the ice in a turn.

The boot will not touch the ice.

The blades are curved.

The curve helps the skater in the turns.

Short track skating is an Olympic medal event.

It has been since 1988.

It is a popular sport.

China and Korea have won many skating medals.

▲ (By Ralf Roletschek (talk) - Fahrradtechnik auf fahrradmonteur.de (Own work)
[CC BY-SA 3.0 at (http://creativecommons.org/licenses/by-sa/3.0/at/deed.en) or
CC BY-SA 3.0 (http://creativecommons.org/licenses/by-sa/3.0)], via Wikimedia Commons)

Figure Skating, the Oldest Event

Figure skating is the oldest of all the events at the Winter Olympic Games. (Aha!)

It was in the 1908 and 1920 Summer Olympic Games.

In 1924, it moved to the Winter Olympics.

It has been a part of every Winter Olympics since then.

Jackson Haines loved music.

He loved dancing.

He was a ballet dancer.

He also loved skating.

He wanted to bring them together.

Americans did not like his new type of skating.

He went to Vienna, Austria.

This town is famous for its music.

It has ice for skating.

There he invented the international style of figure skating.

▲ Jackson Haines
(an American ballet dancer and figure skating genius)

KEY WORDS

- figure skating
- dancing
- ballet dancer
- **bring together** (bring-brought-brought)
- American
- Vienna
- Austria
- be famous for
- invent

Have you seen figure skaters dance on the ice?

They skate to music.

They look graceful.

They make figure skating look easy.

But it is very hard.

Figure skaters must be strong.

KEY WORDS

- Have you seen ~?
- dance
- graceful
- easy

In 1921, the United States Figure Skating Association was formed.

They made rules about jumps and turns.

Some of the moves are named after the people who invented them.

The Axel jump is one. **Aha!**

It is named after Axel Paulsen.

The skater jumps from a forward position.

He lands on the back of the skates.

▲ (By Axel_Paulsen_jump_without_text.png: ErikHK derivative work: Nellinka (Axel_Paulsen_jump_without_text.png) [CC-BY-SA-3.0 (http://creativecommons.org/licenses/by-sa/3.0/) or GFDL (http://www.gnu.org/copyleft/fdl.html)], via Wikimedia Commons)

KEY WORDS

- the United States
- association
- be named after
- Axel jump
- land

Other skating moves are spins.

One is the camel spin.

The skater leans and puts a leg out.

The sit spin is another.

The skater squats low and puts a leg out.

In the upright spin, the skater stands and spins.

There are many more types of moves in skating.

Figure skating boots are custom made.

They have stiff ankles.

They are padded inside.

This protects skaters' feet when they jump.

The blades are made of tempered steel.

This keeps them sharp.

The fronts of the blades have teeth on them.

The teeth grip the ice when the skaters stop.

It helps when they make jumps.

- camel spin (*cf.* camel)
- lean
- put out (put-put-put)
- sit spin
- squat
- low
- upright spin (*cf.* upright)
- custom made
- stiff
- ankle
- inside
- tempered steel
- teeth

Figure skating is like ballet.

In ballet, costumes and music are important.

In figure skating, they are important, too.

It is an artistic performance.

Skaters have rules to follow about costumes and music.

In speed skating, the winners have the fastest time.

In figure skating, judges score many different things.

The skater with the highest score wins.

The Winter Sports Week
in Chamonix, France, was
a success.
More than 10,000 people
paid to see the games.
There were nine different
types of sports.
There were 258 athletes. **Aha!**
247 were men.
Only 11 were women.
That was the start of our
modern Winter Olympics.

▲ a poster for the First Winter Olympics,
which were originally called "International
Winter Sports Week," held in 1924
in Chamonix, France
(By Auguste Matisse (1866 – 1931)
[Public domain or Public domain],
via Wikimedia Commons)

KEY WORDS

- costume
- important
- artistic
- performance

- follow
- score
- highest
- Chamonix

- France
- more than
- pay
- modern

▲ the 2014 Russia Winter Olympics mascots
(By Russian Post, Publishing and Trade Centre "Marka"
(И Т Ц 《М а р к а》). The design of the souvenir sheet by
O. Shushlebina. Scanned by Dmitry Ivanov. (From a personal
collection.) [Public domain], via Wikimedia Commons)

Compare that to the 2014 Winter Olympics in Sochi.

Over 1.1 million tickets were sold.

There were 2,800 athletes.

More than 1,120 were women.

There were 98 events.

There were 15 different types of sports.

The Winter Olympics have changed over the years.

But they still celebrate sports!

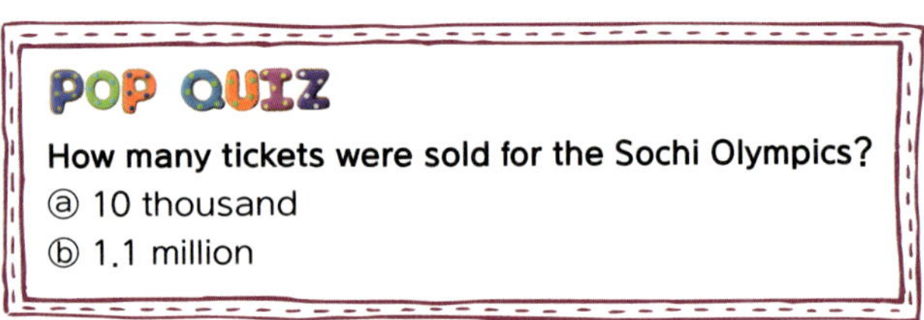

KEY WORDS

- compare
- Sochi
- million
- ticket
- be sold (*cf.* sell (sell-sold-sold))
- change
- over the year
- still

Chapter Four

Comprehension Quiz

A Connect each sporting event and an item related to it.

Long track speed skating

Short track speed skating

Figure skating

❶ •   • a) music

❷ •   • b) clap blade

❸ •   • c) cut proof suit

B Mark T for true or F for false.

❶ In long track speed skating, skaters race against the clock.   T F

❷ The long track speed skating rink is 200 meters long.   T F

❸ The fastest skater wins in speed skating, but in figure skating the highest score wins.   T F

❹ Jackson Haines invented the international style of figure skating.   T F

C Choose the best answer to each question.

❶ Why do long track speed skaters wear colored bands around their upper arms?

a) to show they are past winners

b) to show which team they are on

c) to show which lane they are in

d) to show they are referees

❷ Why are the blades for short track speed skating off-center and on the left of the skate?

a) The curve is pretty.

b) They are less expensive.

c) They last longer than straight blades.

d) They help the skater in the turns.

❸ In figure skating, the costumes and music are important. Why?

a) It is an artistic performance.

b) The audience loves a fancy costume.

c) The music makes everyone happy.

d) The Olympic judges like to listen to music.

Let's Review the Story

Fill in the blanks to review the story.

Title: Skis, Sleds, and ______ !

Skiing

- Cross country skiing: Cross country skiers use skis and p______ to move quickly across the ______.
- Biathlon: The biathlon skier with the ______ time is the winner.
- Ski ______: Jan Bokloev was the first person to put his skis into a "______" shape.

Sledding

- Bobsleigh: The riders ______ the sled back and forth before the race starts.
- Skeleton: Skeleton sleds have b______ on the front and back.
- Luge: The riders lie on their ______ and go down the track feet first.

Curling and Ice Hockey

- Curling: Curling is also called " c______ on ice."
- Ice hockey: The hockey player that guards the goal is a ______.

Skating

- Long track speed skating: Skaters wear special skates that are about ______ centimeters long.
- Short track speed skating: Skaters must wear ______ proof suits to protect themselves from other skaters' ______.
- Figure skating: There are rules about how a skater performs jumps and t______ in a figure skating performance.

Let's Think & Talk

Think about the following questions and answer them freely.

❶ Organize the features of the Winter Olympic sports in the book correctly. Choose the most interesting one and tell us why.

❷ Besides the Winter Olympic sports in the book, check out more sports in the Winter Olympics.

❸ If you could learn one of the Winter Olympic sports, which sport would you want to learn? Why?

Let's Review the Story

Title: Skis, Sleds, and Skates !

Skiing

- Cross country skiing: Cross country skiers use skis and poles to move quickly across the snow .
- Biathlon: The biathlon skier with the fastest time is the winner.
- Ski jumping : Jan Bokloev was the first person to put his skis into a " V " shape.

Sledding

- Bobsleigh: The riders bob the sled back and forth before the race starts.
- Skeleton: Skeleton sleds have bumpers on the front and back.
- Luge: The riders lie on their backs and go down the track feet first.

Curling and Ice Hockey

- Curling: Curling is also called " chess on ice."
- Ice hockey: The hockey player that guards the goal is a goalie .

Skating

- Long track speed skating: Skaters wear special skates that are about 42 centimeters long.
- Short track speed skating: Skaters must wear cut proof suits to protect themselves from other skaters' blades .
- Figure skating: There are rules about how a skater performs jumps and turns in a figure skating performance.

Smart Readers: **Wise & Wide**

After-reading Test

- Skis, Sleds, and Skates!
- Level 2
- 19 Questions

(Vocabulary 5 / Reading Comprehension 10 /

Sentence Structure & Grammar 4)

1. Which pair has the wrong past tense form of the listed verb?
   ① come − came
   ② send − sent
   ③ wear − wore
   ④ spread − spreaded

2. Which pair has the wrong comparative form of the listed word?
   ① fast → faster
   ② long → longer
   ③ light → lighter
   ④ far → farer

※ Choose the right word for each blank. (3~4)

3. Sometimes they bump __________ each other.
   ① of   ② into
   ③ from   ④ toward

4. This is different __________ a long track.
   ① off   ② away
   ③ from   ④ into

5. **What is the common word for the two blanks?**

> • The first bobsleighs were made __________ wood.
> • They sweep the ice in front __________ the stone.

① up   ② on
③ with   ④ of

6. **How many sports were there in the First Winter Olympics?**
    ① six   ② nine
    ③ twelve   ④ nineteen

7. **What are two of the possible penalties if a biathlon skier misses hitting a target?**
    ① run an extra lap
    ② ski an extra lap
    ③ add one minute to his time
    ④ add two minutes to his time

8. **How fast can a bobsleigh go?**
    ① 25 km an hour
    ② 50 km an hour
    ③ 100 km an hour
    ④ 150 km an hour

9. Why do the shoes for the skeleton have spikes on them?
   ① to look sporty
   ② to kick the wall in the turns
   ③ to look more like a skeleton
   ④ to dig into the ice when they get a running start

10. In what year was the first international luge race?
   ① 1838   ② 1883
   ③ 1938   ④ 1983

11. How much do curling stones weigh?
   ① 9.91 kg   ② 19.96 kg
   ③ 99.1 kg   ④ 199 kg

12. How many players does an ice hockey team have on the ice?
   ① 2   ② 4
   ③ 6   ④ 8

13. Which does NOT explain the clap blade?
    ① It snaps into place.
    ② It stays on the ice when the skater moves his foot.
    ③ It helps the skater go faster.
    ④ It helps the skater stop.

14. How long is the short track speed skating rink?
    ① 11.2 meters long
    ② 11.12 meters long
    ③ 111.12 meters long
    ④ 1111.2 meters long

15. Which is NOT a figure skating spin?
    ① Axel   ② camel
    ③ sit   ④ upright

※ Choose the wrong part of each sentence. (16~17)

16.
Then, in 1985, a skier named Jan Bokloev did different something.
       ①   ②   ③   ④

17.

> The goalie tries <u>to stop</u> the puck <u>from</u> <u>go</u> <u>into</u> the goal.
>   ①   ② ③ ④

※ **Choose the right sentence. (18~19)**

18. ① Skiers uses poles help themselves to go faster.
    ② Skiers use poles to help themselves go faster.
    ③ Skiers use poles to help themselves going faster.
    ④ Skiers uses poles to help themselves to going faster.

19. ① The skeleton used been an event for man.
    ② The skeleton used to being an event for man.
    ③ The skeleton used to been events for man.
    ④ The skeleton used to be an event for men.

Suzanne Pitner
Suzanne Pitner is a teacher and writer who has enjoyed visiting Alaska, exploring Rome, teaching in China, and is looking forward to more world travel. She has a Master's Degree in Education, and is a graduate of the Long Ridge Writer's Group. In addition to writing educational articles and books, she writes historical fiction and contemporary fiction for young adults using the pen name Suzanne Lilly.

Skis, Sleds, and Skates!

Written by Suzanne Pitner
Illustrated by Gyeongho Jeong

First Published in April 2017

Editorial Manager: Juyon Choi
Editors: Kyunghee Jang, Jiyeong Park
Designer: Eunhee Lee
Cover Designer: Eunhee Lee

Published and distributed by

 Happy House

Darakwon Bldg., 64-1 Jandari-ro, Mapo-gu, Seoul, Korea 04031
Tel: 82-2-736-2031(ext. 250)   Fax: 82-2-732-2037
Homepage: www.ihappyhouse.co.kr
Publisher: Kyudo Chung

ISBN: 978-89-6653-524-8 18740 / 978-89-6653-156-1 18740(set)

[Components]
• 1 Audio CD (Recording Studio: Aram)
• Answer Keys & Korean Translation: Free download at www.ihappyhouse.co.kr